DID THE TWENTIES ROAR?

THE ROARING 20S & GREAT DEPRESSION IN AMERICA

DID THE TWENTIES ROAR?

THE ROARING 20S & GREAT DEPRESSION IN AMERICA

Sandi Ludwa

By Sandi Ludwa

Ashes to Incense: Emancipation from Jim Crow

Our America: Discovery Through Our Civil War

ISBN: 978-1-7335778-3-0

Dedicated

to the two Annas,
Joseph, Frank, and Nick

Contents

Forward

Do you ever wonder why many older people are virtually misers? Sure, we all like to save money and look for bargains and sales. Some of us regularly shop in thrift stores. Other folks are a mix of both bargain hunter and spendthrift.

My grandma often talked about the old days and hardships the family endured during the Great Depression. She talked about coming to America in 1906 from the Old Country along with grandpa. They were expecting their first child and grandma was very nervous that the authorities would discover their secret and send her back.

They made it into America, became citizens, and survived the Great War, but there were hardships. In 1914, the Scarlet Fever epidemic took one of their three children, and when grandpa was killed after being run-over by a streetcar, grandma had to fend for herself. She assessed her situation. This young immigrant, now a widow of modest means, no formal education, and two young children, found the faith and courage to embrace what she had and build a future for herself and her young offspring.

The 1920s afforded many opportunities. Taking in 'boarders' was one way, and prohibition offered yet another means to survival. Her 'soft drink parlor' on Chicago's West Side turned out to be a great success.

America had enough of the struggles in the first two decades of the Twentieth Century. There had to be an escape from the War and its aftermath, the Influenza pandemic, and constant self-sacrifice that was expected. Now, Lady Liberty escaped and celebrated in the twenties.

But, there was a downside to carefree living. The unpredictable and freewheeling twenties led to the bleak realties of the thirties and the Great Depression. I listened to my mother and grandma tell stories and slowly understood their reasoning and why they hung onto stubborn beliefs and values. All of us, are products of our families, experiences, and environment, and we learn more as we look into history and what went before us. There are lots of stories out there and this one is an over-all look at what Americans faced during these times.

There are many unanswered questions. What led up to our plight in the thirties? Did abandoning Demon Booze ensure a better life? Did the twenties roar or purr? We certainly enjoyed ourselves until we crashed, close to a century ago. In today's world we often ask, "Is our economy headed for another Great Depression?"

You alone are the judge. Come and join me for a trip through the twenties and thirties in America and understand first-hand what Americans went through. This is a book to be enjoyed and provides a simple understanding of this period from post-World War I through the beginning of World War II. This is America's story. It is Our story.

Take my hand, and let's fast-forward to the end of the Great War, World War I. Hang on…

Chapter 1

The Great War is Over—

The Doughboys Come Home

"Over There"
Send the word, send the word to be-ware
We'll be over, we're coming over
And we won't come back till it's over
Over there

George M. Cohan
1917

It was the 11th hour, on the 11th day, in the 11th month…and the Great War was over. The year was 1918. The war had taken its toll of over forty million casualties. If that wasn't sobering enough, the Spanish Flu was still raging and would continue until the summer of 1919 when the pandemic ceased. Another three to five percent of the world population was gone, with estimates in raw numbers ranging up to 500,000 million. La Grippe had also taken its toll.

We were the saviors, had rescued the Allies, and now our veterans were coming home. Some waited until 1919 when they could secure a place aboard a ship for their return. Thousands came back as 'remains' while thousands permanently rested in Europe. Of the living, some were crippled, maimed, or permanently disabled, both mentally and physically. What did they find when returning to our shores? What changed and what stayed status-quo?

Thomas Woodrow Wilson was still president. He presented his Fourteen Points which was his vision for a safer and better world at the Paris Peace Conference. The problem was our government never ratified the Treaty of Versailles and Wilson was perceived a failure. America sat on the sidelines and watched as other countries tried a League of Nations. We became spectators, viewing only an intermission before the final act of a Second World War, some twenty years later. America was tired of internationalism and much like after the Civil War, we wanted the 'good ole days' back in our lives.

Women were working in the jobs that were vacated when our men went to war. Minorities had migrated to the North, found work and less discrimination than they did in the South, and put down roots. Yet, for nonwhites coming home, they realized the reality of segregation still existed and would continue throughout their lifetimes. Once again, our prejudices began to show. Nothing had changed.

Shell shock, now PTSD, was widespread. These troubled men fought in the trenches. Nightmares, anxiety, depression, tremors, paralysis, and dozens of other serious afflictions were the norm for over 76,000 veterans. If we were to pick up a newspaper, we would read about the homeless, insane, imprisoned, or suicidal, and would be overcome with a general feeling of hopelessness. Could the government address this and adequately care for our vets?

Certainly, soldiers were greeted with public welcomes, parades, speeches, and cheers, but was it all very superficial? Once the ticker tape parades and hurrahs ended, they asked Uncle Sam, "Where can I get the help and support that I need?" Soldiers who had participated in the war first-hand couldn't and didn't want to relive events, let alone talk about them to those of us who were not there with them in the trenches.

National organizations filled in some of the gaps. The American Legion arose in 1919. It was and remains such a pillar of support, with a current enrollment of well over 2 million members. The Veterans of Foreign Wars or VFW, existed since 1899 when we fought in the Spanish-American War and is going strong today with over 1.7 million members. Local communities rose to the occasion and did what they could.

Some, who survived combat, came home with diseases. Once symptoms set in, a disease like cholera could kill within hours. Flu, Tuberculosis, venereal diseases, and malaria were not uncommon. One hundred years ago, there were no permanent cures, effective medicines, or antibiotics as we know them today. As a matter of fact, the military did nothing to prevent infections or provide long term relief. Condoms were never distributed, shell shocked men were treated and sent right back into battle, and little thought was given to long-term needs as our forces were overwhelmed with shortages of supplies and medical personnel.

The fact remained, we were tired. Americans wanted no more wars and no more self-sacrifice. We needed to get on with our lives.

Gimme a Drink...

The Eighteenth Amendment went into effect on January 17, 1920. Congress actually listened to the numerous women's groups and religious organizations, such as the Christian Temperance Society, and was ready to enact change. It was a time in our history that women thought they had a voice and were finally being heard. Paychecks were cashed and spent before drunken husbands made it home through the front door. The ladies were fed-up. The Eighteenth Amendment became a part of our Constitution when it passed and this experimentation made the manufacture, sale, and transport of liquor illegal. However, it wasn't illegal to drink.

Why did our government do it? There was a system of logic and it was considered the "Noble Experiment," with its intention to help humanity. The logic flowed this way. If no hard stuff was available, people wouldn't get drunk and squander their last dimes on this Demon Booze. Then, their families would benefit because they weren't deprived of their sustenance. The final result would be that the benefits would flow into the greater good for society. There would be less corruption, improved work habits with greater productivity, less spousal abuse, a huge reduction in violent crime, and everyone would live a healthy life filled with vim, vigor and vitality!

If we solved these social problems, taxes could be reduced, our tax dollars wouldn't be paying for prisons or institutions helping the addicted, and the taxpayer would save money. Sounds good, on the surface, but was it?

It didn't make sense to a lot of Americans, including my grandma who ran her 'soft drink parlor.' Many believed the government had no right to tell them they couldn't drink. They didn't take the precise interpretation which said it was illegal to "manufacture, transport, sell" but not actually 'drink.' These words meant, "How will I obtain my booze?" Afterall, we could still drink, but we'd have to work a little bit harder to find the stash.

People asked, "Why would my government want to regulate my own personal consumption? That's strictly my business." Well, America wasn't exactly the melting pot of lore in the early and mid-nineteenth century.

Since America was largely immigrants, alcohol was and remained a part of various ethnic cultures, and home-brewed beer, mulled wine, and distilled spirits were easily prepared and obtainable. People were now filled with this vim, vigor, and vitality and became very creative.

Liquor produced by the light of the full moon, became moonshine. Sacramental wine was exempt from government control and the demand for it increased remarkably during the first few years of this experiment. More and more Americans attended services at churches and temples throughout the country and the number of self-professed clergy and rabbis grew. God bless America!

Have you ever thought about growing grapes? Lots of vitamins are readily available. Add a bit of sugar, yeast, and be patient. Never let anything go to waste and use those big dandelions growing in your back yard. Make sure that the dandelions are fresh and untainted, however.

There was the downside, and thousands of Americans died from imbibing contaminated alcohol. The same held true for too much alcohol, and at 190 proof, let the drinker beware.

Congress passed the Volstead Act over President Wilson's veto. The Volstead Act provided for the enforcement of the Eighteenth Amendment to the United States Constitution, also known as the Prohibition Amendment. (Wilson remained president through 1921 but we dealt with prohibition until 1933 and the passage of the Twenty-first Amendment). The Act did have loopholes to get around the experiment. One was allowing the average citizen to produce fermented fruit juice.

Pharmacies could also dispense for medicinal purposes and the number of pharmacists tripled. Do you need a tonic for your indigestion or perhaps you're depressed? For three or four dollars you could usually secure a physician's prescription and for another few dollars have it filled.

This "Noble Experiment" failed but it certainly helped business for gangsters. Bootlegging became a lucrative business. It was a new career opportunity, which bred new innovation to make money.

You ask, "How did we allow this to happen?" There was a lot of support as religious and women's groups promoted it, but many Americans felt helpless and believed there was little they could do to prevent passage. The Great War fueled hate against the Germans and names such as Pabst or Schlitz raised bright red flags about the American beer industry. Still, most Americans were unconcerned at the time and let the law pass.

Prohibition was nothing new. As early as 1838 in Tennessee, and Maine in 1851, strict laws were passed and they stayed in effect for long periods of time. In America today, there are still over 80 'dry' counties. Reasons vary from majority religious beliefs, to areas where alcohol abuse is widespread. Some states, however, do prohibit the existence of dry counties or regulate liquor policies.

Laws were and are, one thing, but enforcement is another.

The Speakeasy, Sex, Booze, & Politics

Teddy Roosevelt liked to use the "Speak softly and carry a big stick," phrase, but now the word was, "Speak softly and get a big drink." Teddy's version comes from an old West African proverb.

How did speakeasy's work? In large cities it became a huge business and expanded employment for those in the entertainment trade. Not everyone was welcome and a patron had to be recognized, or know the secret password, handshake, or knock. It was word-of-mouth and who you knew. Small speakeasy's or soft drink parlors could be anywhere. An establishment could be in your neighbor's garage with entry through the back-alley, your summer cottage up at the lake, attics, basements, and places you would never suspect. Mobsters set up their elaborate establishments behind facades of floral shops, bakeries, or any other reputable business.

As police tried to crack down, cards became common. No credit cards in this wallet! Compare it to the present day when we have our private clubs computerized, keeping those who are not part of the group outside of the doors. Cards gave you membership and admission. These were social gatherings and faces were usually familiar ones.

It was a little bit more than knocking on a door and saying, "Joe sent me," and more discretion was involved. There was more discretion. Police could be honest cops protecting the law or those that were on the take and looked the other way.

If nothing else, the number of bars increased rather than decrease. There was no need to buy an expensive license but simply open up your garage or basement. Everyone knew someone who could supply them with the product. Moonshine was popular, powerful, and easy to obtain.

Drinks became cocktails because the booze was so strong. We regulate alcohol on 'proof' which goes back to the British. A proof is how much alcohol is in a beverage and is twice the alcohol content. For example, if you ordered a straight whiskey which had 75% alcohol, the proof was 150%. Since the liquor was so strong, it had to be mixed with other ingredients to tone it down or one could have a heck of a hangover in a few quick sips. Manhattans, Stingers, and Gin Rickey's were born. Social classes now mixed and women gained some freedom if they chose to participate.

Keep in mind, if you lived close to the Canadian Border, you could get your fix from Canada. Our prohibition helped the Canadian economy as it was not illegal to export from the country. Just don't get caught here. Sure, prices were inflated and you could pay about ten times the actual cost of purchase in the North, but after all, we were helping the Canadian economy. Most of the contraband came in through Detroit and Windsor, Ontario. This was well before the Detroit-Windsor Tunnel which was dedicated in 1930.

Did the Twenties Roar?

These 'racy' women who participated in the fun were called "flappers." What did they look like? They wore lighter weight and short dresses with lower waist-lines. Boas adorned their colorful costumes. Sexy and shocking, these ladies wore fancy stockings and short boots that flapped when they danced. Yahoo! Bobbed hair and make-up followed. Heavily rouged checks and bright red lipsticked lips made their debut. Heaven forbid…women smoked and some used cigarette holders! Lordy, Lordy…they drank, and had a good time. Some even abandoned their corsets and swore!

America was "Going to hell in a handbasket," reformers shouted.

The fact remained, we weren't done yet!

Many flappers became overnight successes and our nation followed their every move. Some of these ladies included Clara Bow, also known as the "It Girl," Norma Shearer, and Joan Crawford. A few made the transition into the talkies. The talkies were movies that had soundtracks and were no longer silent. The silent movies had the annoying intertitles or title cards which you had to read quickly in order to get the idea of what was happening.

Nevertheless, social changes were coming fast and furious. When government told Americans what they could or should not do, we displayed our determination to change. We freed ourselves from Great Britain a century and a half prior when we were tired of being a colony and told what to do and how to do it, but now we were faced with rapid social changes and Americans were hungry to gulp them down.

If morality was going downhill, according to some, movies pushed and prodded us down the pathway to hell even more quickly. Movies implied sexual innuendos which included homosexuality, mixed race couples, prostitution, infidelity, and unnatural sex acts. Then there were the drugs, profanity, and stereotypes to contend with. Early movies were tame in contrast to today's standards.

Nevertheless, audiences were enamored with Rudolph Valentino in movies such as *The Sheik* and Louise Brooks in *Pandora's Box*, both quite risqué for the times. When Valentino unexpectedly died in 1926, a line of female mourners patiently waited in a procession that extended for over a mile. They wanted just one last glimpse at the man who had enriched their dreams for the past half-dozen years. His 31 years were filled with scandals, yet almost 100 years later, women still know the name *Valentino*.

We're still in the twenties but slowly into the next decade, regulations and control started seeping into our lives to protect America's traditional values. For now, however, the twenties keep on roaring.

Roar.....

Birth Control

Margaret Sanger opened the first birth-control clinic in 1921. Conservatives, appalled that she started distributing the new form of birth prevention, diaphragms, went through every means to discredit and destroy her. They were ruthless. Although a large majority of both men and women welcomed a method of reliable birth control, Sanger was forced to flee from the United States and went to Great Britain until 1915. She had been arrested for obscenity!

Sanger was a nurse and was familiar with all too many slipshod abortions that destroyed lives. She was also starkly aware of the consequences of numerous and frequent births. Margaret's parents were Irish-Catholic and mother Anne bore eleven children and endured seven miscarriages.

Sanger, like many of her acquaintances, was no saint and lived a very full and active life. Although arrested once again along with her sister, this determined female continued her search for a magic pill. The pill wasn't perfected until 1960, but earlier forms of control were now on the market and added to the easy-living during this age.

Unwed mothers brought shame to families. To be branded with 'illegitimate,' was unacceptable. Many shotgun weddings occurred or women were sent away to maternity homes, children subsequently placed in orphanages, or illegal abortions were performed. Women were constantly reminded of good morals. Catholic girls were faced with the dreaded confessional.

Dr. Sigmund Freud also came up with a few new theories and people seemed to interpret them any way they wanted to. Would suppression of an instinct, such as sex, cause physical disabilities? I think one of its consequences was pimples, or was it insanity?

Sex, booze, and politics were in the forefront. There were even rumors that the Kennedy family made their millions solely from powerful Joseph P. Kennedy's bootlegging. Apparently, during the Nixon administration, Mr. Nixon had started an investigation to dig up evidence of this, in order to use it against John F. Kennedy in the upcoming 1960 election. Other sources claimed to have overheard conversations. It was all hearsay and nothing was proven. The only connection was that Joe's father ran a Boston saloon, before the Eighteenth Amendment was enacted in 1919.

Capone and Gangsters

Perhaps one of the most famous gangsters is Al Capone. Let's go back to this era. Alphonse Capone, was the son of Italian immigrants and born in 1899 in Brooklyn, New York. The family of ten was poor and lived in a New York City tenement. In the sixth grade, Capone had a physical confrontation with his school principal. Capone had been beaten. He struck back at the authority, and abruptly left the New York City Public School System.

When the family moved to a better Brooklyn neighborhood, he met his future wife, Mary Mae Coughlin, and his life-long mentor, Johnny Torrio. Torrio relocated to Chicago but kept intimate ties with his old neighborhood. Capone joined a street gang but overall kept respectable employment, for a while.

However, when he turned 18, his old friend Torrio introduced him to Frankie Yale. Young Capone became a bartender and bouncer at the Harvard Inn in Coney Island. He earned his designation of Scarface soon after, when he was slashed by a patron after making an uncalled for remark to the assailant's sister.

At 19, he married Mary Mae after the birth of their son, Albert. The couple moved to Baltimore where the uneducated Capone worked as a bookkeeper. Apparently, a sixth grade education was all that was needed. When his father passed, Torino brought him to the Windy City, Chicago.

Capone became a bookkeeper for Torino's gambling, prostitution, and new venture…bootlegging. The whole Capone family moved to Chicago, including younger brothers and a sister. Chicago, at this time, had a long history of corruption and Capone was soon involved in politics and payoffs. Mentor, Torino, moved back to Italy and told young Al to lay low for a while. Not Capone…his lifestyle improved, his operations generated approximately $100 million yearly, and he lived high on the food chain.

By this time, Capone learned the value of security and invested in an armor plated Cadillac. American ingenuity had created a lot of new inventions and young Capone had the latest. Bulletproof glass, a police radio, flashing lights, and a huge engine completed his vehicles. He soon had two vehicles. The Capones were a two-car family.

Wonder what happed to Alfonse? When authorities can't pin a specific crime on someone, they usually go after tax records. It was the same in 1931. In 1931, he was convicted of tax evasion and sent to prison in Atlanta. Capone was treated royally, much to the consternation of the feds. Before long, he was transferred to Alcatraz.

Alcatraz Today

Prohibition was dead by the time of his release but the mob still reigned. He was freed for "good behavior" in 1939, suffering from syphilis, and died in 1947.

This was the era of John Dillinger, Joey Gallo, the Gotti's, and Sam Giancana. Forgive me, if I haven't mentioned you, but every large city had its individuals, too numerous to list all. Many turn up in the news in much later years, such as Sam Giancana during the Kennedy administration. Beware, however, Eliot Ness and the Untouchables were out there fighting for law and order!

Our First Woman President?

Did we have a secret president from 1919 through 1921? Although Wilson was still officially president through 1921, he suffered a massive stroke in 1919 and Edith (Bolling Galt) Wilson took control. Woodie, as affectionately called by Edith, had allowed Edith to sit in on meetings from the beginning of their union in 1915. Woodie and Edith had been involved when he was married to his first wife Ellen who died a little over a year before Woodie and Edith wed. There was another woman in the mix also, Mary Peck, but we'll leave that story for another day.

Nevertheless, Woodie courted Edith, they tried to keep their engagement secret, and were successful at keeping reporters away from the wedding. Like many presidents before him, Woodie was never happy with the way the press treated him and there were still rumors, "Did Ellen really die of Kidney Disease and depression, or did he and Edith murder her?" Nothing came of the accusations.

At any rate, after Woodie was incapacitated, Edith ran the whole show. She chose who would be allowed to visit him and make their pitch, sent out press releases, and ran the government. Woodie's health was not in the 'face of the public' until around 1920 when it couldn't be hidden from the common man and woman and the facts were 'leaked' to the American population. This was one hundred years ago in 1919-1920!

As a result, many matters were left to his department heads. We don't know how many decisions this First Lady controlled but our Executive

11

Branch of government was on an autopilot mode. However, such genes Mrs. Wilson professed! She asserted direct descendancy of the elite ruling classes. This included Pocahontas and some type of relationship with both Martha Washington and Thomas Jefferson. Edith considered herself a steward of the presidency and although not elected, well-qualified for the post, more so than Vice President Thomas Marshall, who had been with Wilson through both terms.

A New President – A Return to Normalcy

"A Return to Normalcy," was Warren G. Harding's campaign slogan in 1920, but would it happen? Harding, born in 1865, the same year the Civil War ended in America, witnessed a rapidly changing America and literally employed the French, Laissez les bon temps rouler, which translated means "let the good times roll." The response is, "Oui cher," or something close to that which roughly means, "Yes, my dear."

And…the good times did roll. Harding loved booze, sex, and fun. His administration overflowed with political scandal. Although America was dry, the White House wasn't. Carry Phillips, Nan Britton, and dozens of unnamed acquaintances were on the scene. Britton bore Harding a child, which came to light decades later. If the walls in the White House could talk, they would have plenty to say.

Harding served for barely a year and a half until his untimely death in 1923. There was scandal from day one, but the economy was still booming so we didn't pay a lot of attention. There was mass production. Model-T Fords jumped off the assembly line every 10 seconds and they were affordable for most Americans, including Henry Ford's workforce. Nowadays, we get the manufacturer or dealer discounts, but this was the beginning of the marketing idea. American workers took pride in the product they were building, were happy with their wages, and were grateful for their jobs.

Wages and sales went up. The auto brought freedom, convenience, and mobility. People could live almost anywhere within a huge urban area, on the outskirts of town, or anywhere with accessible roadways. People carpooled as they commuted to cities.

Did the Twenties Roar?

Families took leisurely country drives on Sunday afternoons just for the sake of driving and looking at the scenery, without a sense of urgency to get somewhere quickly. Hop into the auto, plop the kids in the rumble seat, pack a lunch, and off you go.

Soon, the value of roads and paving were a priority as people demanded more and more. This also brought traffic lights, signage, rules, regulations, and traffic tickets. Another new industry surfaced in New York decades ago in the early 1900s and still flourished with the numbers growing. It was the taxicab. America was now mobile!

Make no mistake, America was still a country of have and have nots. As cities grew in size, the suburb developed. People living in the heart of cities often couldn't afford vehicles other than perhaps a bicycle, and still lived in crowded tenements. Then there was a question of parking the vehicle, if you were fortunate enough to own one, without fear of envy or theft. No anti-theft devices in those days! Public transportation was used by virtually everyone, allowing freedom to commute, explore, and socialize.

Nothing has changed. States found new sources of income in motor fuel taxes and vehicle personal property taxes. The dollars generated were used to build and maintain highways and allow the highway system to eventually become self-supporting. Then, as now, the condition of roadways led some to ask, "Where did my taxes go?"

The idea and implementation of the Interstate System was still over three decades away. However, on Veterans Day in 1926, Route 66 was established. Called "The Mother Road," it gave Americans a lifeline and they could travel from Chicago to Santa Monica. Along the route, businesses sprung up as people migrated westward.

In other industries, e.g., aviation, chemicals, broadcasting, movies, big banks, and national food chains, growth was by leaps and bounds while others were driven out of business. There still existed, however, the corner stores, butcher shops, bakeries, and small town conveniences. We knew the butcher, baker, and candlestick maker and often could still get our groceries put on a "tab" that we would pay off on payday. However, then, as now, it was becoming more and more difficult for a small entrepreneur to survive against the already established conglomerates. All of us liked our local A & P (Atlantic & Pacific Tea Company), Piggly Wiggly, and National (Tea Co.) where we could buy a huge variety of foods.

Corporations called for "open shops" or the breaking of union contracts. They instituted the American Plan which bullied employers. Employers didn't want organized unions and pressured workers to keep things as they were. Employees knew they were expected to reject membership or suffer consequences. Consequences were not just warnings, but there were strong-arm tactics. The old movies show us these ploys fully-detailed. There were mixed feelings. Did paying union dues provide job security, raise wages, and ensure better working conditions overall, or were they a scheme lining the pockets of a few?

As a result, wages remained low, profits skyrocketed, and the birth of 'easy credit' occurred. At the same time, overcapacity of consumer goods existed, and some industries moved South for cheap labor. What a bonanza! Now, many of us had electricity and with it there were new innovations. Refrigerators, electric irons, toasters, and fancy ovens were becoming commonplace. We started wearing sunglasses and wrist watches. Imagine mom's pleasure at finding a new vacuum cleaner under the Christmas tree on Christmas morning! Everything seemed wonderful for a while, but things would soon change.

Farmers were in trouble as there were surpluses and shrinking demand, lower prices, tenant farming, sharecropping, and racism, all lurking and waiting for a chance to pounce. More details on this forthcoming when we enter our depression.

If you had money, no worries if you broke the law and got caught. Harding's appointees sold 'pardons' allowing wealthy friends and enemies alike, to avoid imprisonment. You had only to pick up the newspapers to read the sensationalism of the day.

One of the largest scandals in the administration was the Teapot Dome-lease of petroleum reserves to oil companies in exchange for cash, bonds, and cattle – initiated by Secretary of the Interior Albert Fall. This was the Watergate of the 1920s and as the probe went on, more and more corruption was discovered.

Blackmail, payoffs to the news media, suicides, all involving Harding's cabinet, a.k.a., the Ohio Gang were one huge story of corruption at the highest levels. Harding allegedly asserted that he didn't have any problem whatsoever with his enemies, it was his friends that worried him.

Did the Twenties Roar?

Every dog has his day and Albert Fall did fall, but came out ahead, the way I did the math. He was imprisoned for one year and fined $100,000 although he had taken $385,000 or more in bribes. Will we ever know? Where did the other $285,000 go? The land was returned to our government, and still produces oil, although our government did, in fact, sell it in 2015.

For Sale, Highest Bidder

Harding's time in the White House was so overcome with disgrace, that there was even suggested scandal in his death. When Harding suddenly died there was no autopsy, at Florence Mabel Kling Harding's request. Was it a heart attack, stroke, poisoning, or food poisoning? We know his hemorrhoids were bothering him, he had a fever, and he was taking laxatives.

The president was touring in San Francisco when he succumbed. There were various accounts of his passing. Was Florence reading him a flattering story about himself from the *Saturday Evening Post* or was Florence actually present with him at the time?

Chapter 2

"Keep Cool with Coolidge"

Our Love Affair Continues...or does it?

In the old-days, we wore campaign buttons. We wore them shamelessly and they were freely given away to any interested party. When there was a parade, handfuls travelled through the air from the fancy parade floats. We were unafraid of being assaulted or sneered at when expressing a personal opinion and telling the world who we were going to vote for.

When Harding died of a heart attack, **Calvin Coolidge** was located. He was visiting his father in Vermont. Fortunately, dad was a notary public and swore him in since the Chief Justice was hundreds of miles away.

Coolidge continued the pro-business philosophy. New York City had skyscrapers and the amazing 102 story Empire State Building. Americans were now traveling and Miami Beach became a tourist mecca with its forever sunny skies, hotels, unpolluted beaches, gigantic swimming pools, and well-tanned bodies. Detroit, the Motor City boomed. Coolidge believed America was business and there should be little government interference.

However, since World War I when we became a creditor nation, some things changed. Without American help, the Allies could not have won the war. We sacrificed our men and women, and gave technology, materials, and money. Now, we wanted our money repaid and some European nations wouldn't and couldn't pay. Jobs started moving overseas, and it was none other than Henry Ford who started building plants in Japan and Turkey. There was no going back to a totally "Made in America" nation.

In 1924, the National Origins Act was passed. It targeted annual immigration by a confusing formula that went back to populations in 1890, which favored certain nationalities and excluded others. It was another one of those government acts with too many whys and wherefores that were amended. When Coolidge signed the Act, a.k.a., Johnson-Reed Act, he asserted that our country must strictly be kept American.

To continue our journey into despair…in the South agriculture still reigned after the war and sharecropping was dominant. There was a demise of the general store. Automobiles, roads, and cash only were a thing of the past. The law was on the side of the landowners. There was a depopulation of the South. In rural areas, it seemed to many that the men drank and women were always pregnant. Families were large and there was never divorce, just desertion. Women still had few choices.

The Southern rural areas remained poor and isolated, and there were bugs, ignorance, minimal washing and cleanliness. Despite this, there was often a strong sense of community. Plenty of activities existed. There were 4-H clubs, trips to town, and church-going through circuit ministers and plenty of church involved events.

Mules still pulled coffins and black funerals were held on Sundays. People still stooped over and picked cotton by hand. Prison was often better than home where at least the meals were provided. In addition, there was convict labor. A person could be arrested on any trumped-up charge, placed in prison, and hired out to a local employer with the law enforcement official keeping the revenue. Law and order depended upon the community and the circumstances.

Before we get into the Great Depression, let's change the subject for a minute and do a little traveling. This time it is 1925 and we are going to the Scopes Monkey Trial in a small town in rural Tennessee. It's going to be exciting because it's the Darwinists against the Fundamentalists. This will give us an idea of the many cultures existing in our Roaring Twenties nation.

Religion, Fundamentalism, and Education

American religion by the end of World War I had become a great divide. One divide was the debate over mankind's origins. It was brought to public attention by a well-publicized trial in the tiny hamlet of Dayton, Tennessee in 1925.

Charles Darwin was a British naturalist and biologist who was born on the exact same day as Abraham Lincoln, February 12, 1809. He traveled around the world and recorded his findings, concluding with his theory of evolution. Although Darwin published, *On the Origin of Species,* in 1859, and died in 1882, to mention his Darwinian Theory was a sin to many world-wide. He was condemned by many denominations.

His Theory of Evolution was like politics in the twenty-first century. It was a topic that couldn't rationally be discussed in many communities. The subject of evolution was particularly a no-no in areas where the Southern Baptists dominated. They rejected even the notion that mankind originated from a lower animal ancestry. So publicized, his theory was expanded to include Social Darwinism which tried to explain that government shouldn't interfere with society and should employ a laissez-faire ideal, not helping the poor, different races, and nationalities. This would allow only the fittest to survive.

Yes, the subject is still debated today by scientists, religious, politicians, and everyday Americans on all sides of the issue. However, in 1925 the religious aspect was explosive.

"The Bible has to be interpreted literally," said the Christian Fundamentalists.

"We will interpret God's word for you, listen to us instead," Evangelicals proclaimed.

Billy Sunday continued his Hellfire and damnation oratories that he had been preaching for decades. It was the twenties and there was a battle between figures such as Sunday and Aimee Semple McPherson who preached against the forces of evil: jazz, racy movies, sexual permissiveness, and lack of Christian morals.

The Eugenics movement was also taking hold and caused overwhelming concern. Fortunately, this faction died out in America in the thirties but not in Germany. Eugenicists hoped to improve the human race by discouraging those deemed as undesirable from mating, while encouraging those with desirable traits to procreate.

Catholics and Jews remained silent and formed their own opinions. Some preachers tried to incorporate God's plan into the evolutionary ideas that were rampant.

The Monkey Trial

However, it all came to decision time in March 1925 when Tennessee passed a law banning the teaching of Darwinism in any state-funded school. This was not unusual in twentieth century America, if we look at the fact that in our twenty-first century America, more and more schools are dictating what should and should not be taught. Back in 1925, many parents were simply appalled that their children could explain and justify animal ancestry more thoroughly than they could support Bible teachings. Parents believed their youngsters were being taught to be atheists.

John T. Scopes, twenty-four years old, was a substitute science teacher and part-time coach, who was approached by a prominent town leader who was originally from New York. The American Civil Liberties Union regarded the Tennessee law, the Butler Act, as unconstitutional and advertised it would support anyone willing to test it in court. Scopes, at this time, had been filling in for the Biology teacher and agreed to test the case. He was arrested and the trial was scheduled.

Dayton, Tennessee, July 10, 1925

The town is in Rhea County Tennessee, off of U.S. 27, and in 1925 the population dwindled down to less than 2,000. The area had fallen on hard times.

It was hot and muggy. Holy Rollers lined the countryside and watched intently while caged monkeys were being brought into town to afford some drama to the trial. Rumor had it that these talented and gifted monkeys would indeed testify.

Banners hung everywhere in this small town that had one hotel, unable to accommodate all of the visitors. Copies of T. T. Martin's book *Hell and the High School* were freely distributed, and over 1000 people were crammed into the courthouse alone. The town officials originally planned to set up a tent to house 20,000 people, but the idea was shot down.

Loudspeakers were set up and there was seating in other town buildings. The courtroom was tightly packed while the jury of twelve men was ushered in. For the first time in America's history, the first trial run of a national broadcast occurred that day in the tiny town of Dayton. It was broadcasted through WGN Radio in Chicago and cable-lines were placed between Chicago and Dayton, a distance of over 500 miles.

Dayton, Tennessee Museum

Enter William Jennings Bryan, the Silver-tongued Orator. By this time, Bryan had been in politics for over 30 years but hadn't practiced law during those years. A liberal and strong Fundamentalist who ran for president three times and lost, Bryan looked forward to the event. He now represented Tennessee in *Tennessee v. Clarence Darrow*.

Although Clarence Darrow was now almost 70 years old and an agnostic, he was a prominent lawyer and in demand. He brought with him a distinguished career and a long list of successful high profile cases that he had won. Darrow was victorious in the Leopold, Jr. and Loeb trial, which newspapers called 'The Trial of the Century.' The elderly-Darrow was also a distinguished member of the American Civil Liberties Union. Now, Darrow was representing Scopes and the ACLU.

Darrow knew it would be a circus atmosphere and almost turned down the case, but he figured out that with or without him, this would be the situation. Both sides knew they had adequate defense teams and believed they were on the correct side and would win this war.

They were ready. Both Bryan and Darrow gave their opening speeches but Judge John Raulston wouldn't allow Darrow to talk about evolution. Darrow, not to be outsmarted, figured out a way around this.

Lo and behold, Darrow called Bryan as a witness! He asked him for a literal interpretation of the Bible. The Silver-tongued Orator, Bryan, was tongue-tied and said this was impossible. Embarrassed, Bryan hung his head as Darrow looked jubilant!

Unfortunately, the trial dragged on for eight long and miserable days. The Judge ruled out any scientific testimony on evolution. By the time the trial ended, both Bryan and Darrow were exhausted.

The courtroom was quiet for a change, as everyone was awaiting the final verdict...

The jury was out for a total of nine minutes and had the verdict. Bryan was victorious. Scopes was fined $100, which would be somewhere around $1400 today. This trial also, became another Trial of the Century.

Although the verdict was overturned on a technicality by the Tennessee Supreme Court, it was sensationalism and the teaching of evolution was banned in many states. Scopes, on the other hand, came out ahead. He was given a further education FREE by the University of Chicago where he studied geology and became a petroleum engineer.

Dayton, Tennessee Courtroom today
Scene of the Monkey Trial

Bryan prepared his closing statement. He never used it but planned on using in his future speeches. Unfortunately, the following Sunday after the trial, he died in his sleep. The Butler Act in Tennessee wasn't repealed until 1967!

Sandi Ludwa

The Boulder Dam

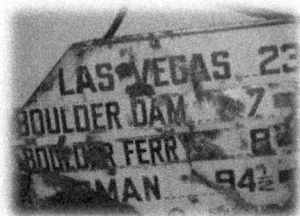

Boulder City Museum

In December 1928, Coolidge did a good thing. He authorized the Boulder Canyon Dam Project. Construction was a God-send in the coming years as we entered the Great Depression. The structure to be built was to be called the Hoover Dam, although it wasn't officially named until after World War II. It was built in Black Canyon on the Colorado River, and encompasses two states, Nevada and Arizona. Its damming of the Colorado River formed our largest Reservoir, Lake Mead. Only one community was destroyed with the flooding. St. Thomas, Nevada was settled by Mormons in 1865, and now it disappeared.

Herbert Hoover was Secretary of Commerce back in 1922 and instituted a Compact to divide the waters of the Colorado River between seven states. The designation was that it would honor Hoover, the next president. Its story is an interesting one. I'll save this Dam Story for later, when we get into the Great Depression.

Lucky Lindy

The 20s wouldn't be complete without mentioning Lucky Lindy. There was the Orteig $25,000 prize for the first pilot to fly from New York to Paris, a distance of 3,600 miles. Other pilots had tried for the bounty but were unsuccessful. One crashed at take-off, another disappeared over the Atlantic, never to be heard from again, and there were other attempts with serious injuries. Orteig ran the contest and no one tried, so he extended it after five years with no takers, hoping someone would take up the challenge. It soon changed because aviation was finally advancing into more reliability and men responded to the call, hoping to win the big prize.

The story goes that it was overcast and rainy on May 20, 1927 as three planes lined up in Long Island. One of the pilots flew the *Spirit of St. Louis*, a tiny craft with NO radio. The fuel was carried in the cockpit. It was piloted by a thin, blond, handsome-twenty-five year old.

There was no communication, since the *Spirit* had no radio, but still crowds awaited. Thirty-three hours later, the lone pilot landed in France and was physically lifted from the cockpit by the crowd. He said, "I am Charles Lindbergh." He hadn't slept in over two days total considering his preflight prep, and experienced hallucinations inflight, but somehow made it.

Five years later he would be in the headlines once again. When his 20 month old son was kidnapped and found dead, it was considered the crime of a century, and the world was shocked. Later he spoke on his views pro-Germany and Hitler and was branded as an anti-Semite and traitor.

I know, many of you are thinking the same thing I did, "How did Lindy go to the bathroom?" Apparently his seat was wicker and it had a hole in it with a funnel attached. The material was deposited into an aluminum can. Lindberg stated he dropped the excrement somewhere over the French countryside. Oh my!

Chapter 3

"A Chicken in Every Pot and a Car in Every Garage"

This takes us to our next president, Herbert Hoover. We're still living in the 20s and roaring along together. The 1928 election campaign was an interesting one, because it involved religion, as well as the major issues. Hoover took office in 1929 running against Roman Catholic Democrat, Alfred E. Smith, the Governor of New York. Coolidge declined running for another term.

Discussion exists to this day as to why Silent Cal declined running. He wrote a short note for the reporters stating the fact, without explanation. As early as 1923 he had stated his intention of not running in 1928. Was he tired of cleaning up the Harding scandals and restoring faith in our government? Some stated it was the deaths of his father and one of his sons, 16 year old, Calvin, Jr. that took the wind from his wings. Could it have been knowledge that a depression would soon begin in earnest? Needless to say, on the date of the announcement, Grace Coolidge appeared surprised when told the news by the press; he had not mentioned the announcement to her that morning.

The field came down to Hoover, the Republican, and the Democrat, Smith. Smith, "the Happy Warrior," had obstacles to overcome in order to convince the American public to give him the vote. People from all walks of life condemned Smith. While popular fundamentalist Billy Sunday condemned Smith, he claimed no animosity against Smith's religion, but he did condemn Smith's choice of associates, calling them names ranging from pimps to liberal bootleggers.

Sunday was handsome, influential, charismatic, and a former major-league baseball player for the Chicago White Stockings, (presently the White Sox). He was a flag-waving American, unafraid of expressing his political, religious, and very personal views. His compelling and passionate voice mesmerized many while he provided both inexpensive entertainment and spiritual inspiration. Sunday provided animated sermons as he constantly moved around as if he were doing an aerobic workout.

One of my favorites of Sunday's quotes involved his statement that attending services on Sundays no more made you a good Christian than walking into a garage would make you an automobile. Sunday was very direct in all of his statements, pulling no punches. He was also a former hard-drinking guy who saw the light, became a preacher for the YMCA, and gave up baseball. He totally endorsed prohibition.

The Happy Warrior, on the other hand, had several other things going against him. He was a moderate social drinker, but campaigned against prohibition. Strikes two and three came quickly because he was also a New Yorker and a Catholic. The rumor circulated that Smith lost the election because people believed he would take orders from the Pope. (The same rumor circulated during the 1960 presidential election when John F. Kennedy, our first Catholic president, ran for the office).

If that wasn't bad enough, Smith worked for a time at New York's Fulton Fish Market, used poor grammar, and had a Lower Eastside accent. People concluded that this was all probably the result of his poor education. The American public read newspapers, spread rumors, believed what they wanted to believe, and passed along their conclusions. Although accusations were cruel, the fact remained, the Republicans were in power. This was the party associated with the booming and "roaring" times, whereas the Democrats were associated with the corrupt Tammany Hall.

There were many groups to satisfy everyone's beliefs but not one could please everyone. Everyone was a part of one of the tribes: prohibitionists, urban workers, rural poor, uneducated, immigrants, Catholics, Protestants, Fundamentalists, or Klansmen. It came down to the Democrats against the Republicans once again.

One strong group, however, reemerged, the KKK. Stronger than fifty years ago, it sought the White Anglo Saxon male. This time, its purpose was not to torment only the blacks, but Catholics, Jews, Latinos, Muslims, immigrants, and every other minority. Advertised as a secret, social, fraternal, American, and patriotic organization for men of high moral standards and character, it grew to over 5 million members.

Sandi Ludwa

Who was this man Hoover?

Herbert Clark Hoover, a Quaker, was orphaned at age nine, and grew up poor. Although he was unwanted, lonely, and shuffled around between relatives, he became a self-made millionaire by the time he turned forty. He was admitted into Stanford's inaugural class after failing the entrance exam and required tutoring. Hoover graduated in 1895. At Stanford he met Lou Henry who was to become his wife. She was the first woman to earn a B.A. in Geology from Stanford.

Hoover worked as a miner in Nevada City for a short period, then moved on to an engineering job, and quickly became successful. The presidency was his first elected office. Prior, he had been appointed to all of his positions. Hoover donated his salary to various charities once he became president and was nominated for the Nobel Peace Prize five times, but was unsuccessful in actually winning the honor.

When we talk about the Great Depression, the name Hoover immediately comes to mind. He received totally negative press in his handling of America during the Great Depression but was credited for his outstanding humanitarian efforts worldwide during and after World War I. As a result of his work in World War I, he formulated his ideas on volunteerism and working together for the greater good, believing this would solve America's problem.

The Hoover administration continued the laissez-faire philosophy, defined as the 'leave us alone attitude.' Many Americans blamed him for the Great Depression but one man alone didn't cause the Depression. The stage was already set and the cast was in place by the time he took office. Hoover preferred to call the Depression a Recession caused by overspeculation in the stock market. You be the judge, what would you have done?

Hoover's catchy slogan was:

"A chicken in every pot and a car in every garage."

But, was there a chicken to be had, or even a bicycle to park in the nonexistent garage? Easy credit was born years ago and cash wasn't needed, but things soon changed.

It seemed like the old saying, "when it rains, it pours," dominated. It wasn't rain but bad weather with drought and crop failures ruining agriculture. This was the era of the Dust Bowl, with no rain, wind-erosion, and the subsequent toll on human health.

Few are still alive who lived through the Great Depression, but many of us can recall hard times. Have you seen Tumbleweed rolling across the roads out West? Well, out of necessity, people in the West, like prairie dogs and mule deer, ate it. They developed ways to cook and eat Tumbleweed or Russian thistle.

We listened to the new-age music with its gentle tempos of the "Jazz Age," and morality changed. While elders asserted that the music and dance would lead all of us to moral ruin, Americans flocked to the dance halls and clubs. We could foxtrot, waltz, tango, or try the new rage, the Charleston.

In the major cities, there was segregation and often races other than white weren't allowed into the establishments, other than furnishing the entertainment. They formed their own organizations. An aside on tensions which existed in Chicago needs to be mentioned. Chicago, Illinois is an example of severe tensions between races in the 1920s resulting in riots and murders. Even though there was no segregation as practiced in the South, (other than public beaches), the influx of southerners pushed the city to its limits with jobs and housing. Displaced southern blacks came in large numbers early in the twentieth century and threatened displacement of white workers from jobs.

However, the 1920s was still the Jazz Age and we came to be entertained. Ethnic groups still lived in their own pockets in the cities and when seeking an evening of entertainment in dance, would tend to congregate with their own by dividing up areas of a ballroom. Notable venues were Chicago (Trianon, Aragon), or New York (Savoy, Cotton Club).

Soon there were taxi dancers. Clubs would employ young and attractive women to dance with men who usually paid ten-cents a dance with pre-purchased tickets. Many women found this a good source of additional income, while parents frowned upon it. Bars and saloons still existed despite prohibition and the speakeasies or private clubs became a lucrative business for mob activity and gangsters, as well as average American entrepreneurs.

Our dresses were now very short and duplicated again in the 1960s when we wore miniskirts, although we didn't go back to the 'bobbed' hair. Heavy make-up with bright red lipstick were the rage along with our rouged checks. Follow-up with a dab of powder and some eye shadow and we're ready for a night on the town! Makeup was relatively cheap but the application to provide a new 'face' took some time. We would frequent the 'powder room' in a restaurant which was just a fancy name for 'bathroom.'

There were the have and the have nots. Half of the population lived below the subsistence level, politicians were corrupt and pushed their own views, blind to their constituents. Did I mention, oligopolies dominated the era? Not only was there no chicken in every pot, but not even a bicycle in every garage. Did anyone even have a house, let alone a garage? People walked everywhere. These conditions continued for years.

Today we are experiencing the plight of the homeless, with tents being raised in parks, on beaches, and in the heart of our large cities. Such was the case a century ago but on a larger scale. The depression affected everyone.

Hard Times for Everyone

Hooverville's, or shanty towns, spread across our America. Oklahoma City, for example, had a shanty town spread out over 100 square miles. People lived in rusty car bodies, orange crates, cardboard shanties, and relied upon the many soup kitchens that fed the unemployed and homeless. People even lived in New York's Central Park. Our old acquaintance, Al Capone opened a Chicago soup kitchen. For some, it was the only food they received all day. Jane Adams' Hull House in Chicago continued to house the homeless in this massive city but efforts were never enough to dig our way out of the situation. It wasn't just the unknown vagrant, but it was everyone.

Hard times took its toll on all classes. People placed their children in orphanages when they couldn't provide for them. Orphan trains had operated since the late 1800s but came to an abrupt end in 1929. This was largely due to state laws which prohibited the movement of children who were sometimes subjected to conditions worst than while in their prior citified environments. Most states adopted family laws and foster care systems by this time.

Farmers went bankrupt and came together to avoid eviction. They formed associations and dumped produce, dairy, and foodstuffs rather than sell at the rock-bottom prices. At one point, beef went down to .01 a pound. Most hoped the government would support a farm program to help them.

There were strikes over wage cuts. The National Guard was often called to assist. People were killed or seriously injured. Everyone wanted some government action.

Let's talk about clothing & garters

Clothing was tattered, torn, and worn until it fell apart. My mother told me how people placed foil, cardboard, or pieces of tires, in their shoes when the soles began to show signs of daylight. Socks were always mended as was clothing. Unlike today's fashion rages of gaping rips and perforations in jeans, as poor as people were, they never wanted to be seen with holes in their clothing.

Hand-me-downs were nonexistent as the clothing became rags before it could be given to the next recipient. Nothing was ever thrown away and flour sacks were a good source of material. Soon, even the sacks had bright and colorful designs, in an attempt for the manufacturers to sell more flour, seed, or feed.

Have you ever cut up your old shirt and made undergarments? This was commonplace. Today our clothing is mass-produced and we can all be stylish without breaking the piggybank, as clothing becomes more affordable. In the 1930s, we did not import most of our clothing from overseas, and yes, sweatshops still existed. The average price of a men's overcoat could be about $15 to $20 in 1930s dollars, and don't forget a flannel robe for about $1 to $4. Considering, if you had a job, you might earn between 10 and 30 cents an hour.

At the beginning of the 1930s, people worked 50 hour weeks, but as jobs became more and more scarce, it went down to 40 hours. Consider working for 30 cents an hour for 40 hours and taking home $12. From this, support your household which usually consisted of more than the nuclear families of today. Birth control was still not 100% reliable. Usually, children lived with their parents, grandparents, and sometimes aunts, uncles, and cousins in the family home. This was, however, if you were fortunate enough to own a home. Thousands upon thousands of men, women, and children took to the streets and the rails. This is where overalls became important. (Read down a couple of paragraphs).

I can remember my grandmother who had a stash of buttons, yes buttons. As a child I was fascinated. She stated she had saved many of them since the 1920s when buttons were becoming scarce. Whenever there was a lost button on a blouse or shirt, she would go into her stash and find one. Whenever we purchased new clothing, she would immediately "tighten" the buttons on the article before we could wear them. This ritual was passed along to my mother but not to me.

For those who could afford some new clothes, the depression changed the way clothing was manufactured. Women used to wear stockings made out of rayon but now the nylon stocking replaced the rayon. Nylon was cheaper. Nylons had seams on them. The colors were darker than skin color and we had to make sure the seams were straight. How were they held up, since pantyhose were nonexistent? Garter belts or garters were used. When using garters, you had to make sure the garter was high enough so it wasn't seen. Yes ladies, brides were not the only ones to wear garters. Instead of long stockings, short anklets could be worn.

Of course, you could simply wear your girdle which could have garters for attachment to stockings. No self-respecting woman would dare venture from her residence without a girdle for fear her behind might wiggle too much. A smooth look was the goal. Now girdles are not to be confused with corsets – the novel piece of apparel Scarlet O'Hara wore to attain her 17 inch waist and attain that hourglass figure. Girdles were from the waist down to the top of the leg, stomach, thigh, and torso.

Times did change and the nylon stocking disappeared when once again our skirts became shorter and shorter. In the 40s when nylon was in short supply, women drew lines down the back of their legs to imitate the stocking seam or line. By the 70s, however, pantyhose became the norm but we now are in the 2020s and many of us don't wear hose at all!

Did the Twenties Roar?

Just one note on women's shoes. If, once again, you had money to buy shoes in the 1930s, there was always a heel, usually high. Women wore them and walked naturally, not on tippy-toes with small carefully planned steps. They didn't worry about falling over with every short step or catching the heel on some grated sidewalk surface. Heels were the fatter version, not close to resembling the skinny heels and platforms of today. They did exist for one reason as well as style, and that is comfort and body support. When the heels or soles felt well-worn, the shoes went to the local shoemaker who would replace the surface with a rubber heel or sole.

For men, a pair of loafers, leather sandals, or work boots would do. Keds were available if you wanted a sneaker for any purpose, both men's and women's sizes. In 1938, there were the Kedettes which were a high heel washable shoe for women. They were advertised for the girl who wanted to be popular. Cute huh? Keds are still around today and stylish, but not meant for serious sports.

Dresses that used to be silk were now rayon, but most wore simple-cotton-housedresses. Working around the house, no one wore jeans but donned housedresses which could be very stylish and made of cotton. There were V-necked cardigans, and wrap-around skirts and yes, hats were still a part of the trousseau. The zipper replaced buttons. Oh, did I mention that most women knew how to sew their own clothing?

Kids usually had play clothes, second bests, and Sunday best clothing. If mom was creative, she would decorate her clothing as well as children's with any tidbits of fabric or buttons. Women had patterns and sewed by hand or with pedal sewing machines.

Men still wore suits and inserted shoulder pads to give them the uniform and square look. Workingmen wore overalls which were a protective clothing, along with a button-down shirt underneath. For those of you who have never worn overalls or aren't familiar with them, they are pants with a chest covering and suspender-like material to hold them in place, one piece. It took longer to get them down so you could go to the bathroom.

Sorry, no pictures in this section.

Sandi Ludwa

Jobs, Corruption, & Politics

Many believed that a woman's place was still in the home and no decent woman should be working at an outside job if her husband was fortunate enough to be employed. Boarders were one source of money, taking in laundry was another, and selling baked goods when able was commonplace. Families once again became 'extended' in order to survive. More black women than white worked because they had taken jobs such as house servants, nannies, or house cleaning, working for whites. It had always been a means of survival and support for black families. The fact was that more women of all groups worked now than ever before. Families needed the income.

However, overall, soon those who had previously taken the undesirable jobs, such as Japanese or Hispanics, were forced out as whites took whatever was available. Some, such as the Chinese, stayed in their own communities and supported one another with restaurants and laundries. There was also a large Mexican influx because no immigration quotas existed for the western hemisphere. Labor was provided for largely agricultural jobs and many returned home once they had earned enough for support. They were considered America's temporary immigrants.

Back to reality…so what caused the Great Depression? Was it the stock market crash of 1929? Many believe that the stock market crash that occurred on Black Tuesday, October 29, 1929 is one and the same with the Great Depression. It was only one of the causes that led to this time in history.

Black Tuesday was actually the fourth and last day of the stock market crash of 1929. Investors had traded a record 16.4 million shares and Black Tuesday kicked-off the Great Depression. By the late 20s, it got to the point where large investors could put down as little as ten percent on margin and purchase stock. It was all a gamble, and sometimes gambling didn't pay-off.

Two months after the original crash in October, stockholders had lost more than $40 billion dollars. Even though the stock market began to pick up a bit, by the end of 1930, it wasn't good enough, and America truly entered what is called the Great Depression.

Did the Twenties Roar?

Abandoned Orange Factory, Florida

We're back to square one. What was and is the cause of a depression? Was it, a reckless stock market, unprecedented growth and extreme wealth for the large corporations? Was this growth accompanied by little diversity in products beyond the basic industries, and families living beyond their means? No doubt, it was an era of "keeping up with the Joneses." Put it on credit and we'll think about paying tomorrow was the norm! Do we ever learn?

Other world economies were developing and the demand for American goods dropped. While countries still owed America for World War I loans and weren't meeting their repayment terms, we solved the problem and gave them even more credit.

Small shop owners were put out of business, unable to collect debts after being forced to give credit. When weather didn't cooperate, farmers took out loans that they were unable to repay. People hit rock bottom when they had to rely on tenancy in farming. Having a decent garden and maybe a cow or a few chickens made a difference.

We are now complacent that banks insure our savings, but not in the 1920s. People had placed their dollars in banks for safe keeping, but soon learned there was no safety and perhaps those dollars should have been kept in the shoe box under the bed. During the 1930s, over 11,000 banks failed. Those that survived stopped giving loans and people stopped buying. There was no need for abundant consumer goods, and we lost jobs. Unemployment went up to twenty-five percent. Wages were cut.

No longer could Americans make their installment plan payments. Items were repossessed. Do you remember a time before credit cards? There was extreme popularity in layaway and will call. We would make payments on an item and once it was paid off, could pick it up at the store. If we could not make payments and cancelled the order, money was refunded less a handling fee. Some viewed it as a savings plan.

Layaway slowly lost its popularity with the advancement of credit cards, as did the appeal of Christmas Clubs which were common in the 1960s and 1970s. It seemed like every bank and credit union sponsored a club. We would place money into an account all-year-long and then take it out around December 1 for our Christmas shopping. In 2011, during a recession, layaway was resurrected by Walmart and many other retailers followed. It exists today.

Historians will ponder that question for decades to come as today we still continue to ask over and over again, "What causes led to our Great Depression?" Will it happen again?

Hoover (remember he was president during the depression) believed in voluntarism, optimism, and never interfered with corporations. October 1929 rolled around and the Stock Market Crash (Black Tuesday). At this time, approximately one percent of the population controlled around forty percent of the wealth in America.

The yellow-press said people jumped out of skyscrapers, off the Brooklyn Bridge, were setting themselves on fire in record numbers, or committed horrific suicides. The story goes that when approached for room rentals, hotel clerks would respond with, "Do you want a room for sleeping or for jumping?" These events were few and far between and most of America worked with what they had, survived, had families, and worked together to build America up once again.

In 1928, Franklin D. Roosevelt was elected Governor of New York. He took the nomination from Smith, who ran unsuccessfully against Hoover for President. FDR didn't want to run, wasn't sure he could win, and hoped to continue his rehabilitation in Warm Springs, Georgia. It wasn't to be.

As governor, FDR learned quickly as he was now facing the Great Depression and upcoming Black Tuesday, in one of the most populous states in the union. He traveled throughout the state, took notes, and talked to the common man. The Progressive governor developed his belief that government needed to take a stronger stance in everyone's lives. He called his programs his social duties.

During his two terms, FDR tackled corruption and Tammany Hall, reformed the state's prison system (Attica was built), developed hydroelectric power for the state, and started a relief system to stimulate public employment. Perhaps his biggest challenge was fighting the long-term corruption that existed for centuries. Teddy Roosevelt had faced the same situation decades earlier as a Republican.

Patronage

Let me talk a little about large cities and political patronage. I grew up in Chicago, which illustrates a prime example of it. The area in which I lived was strongly Democrat. After all, the last Republican mayor was in 1927 when Big Bill Thompson was elected. I really don't know if there were any Republicans at all, but as a kid, this is what I remember.

Whenever anyone on our block needed a favor or something to be done quickly, they called the "Precinct Captain." This could be a streetlight fixed, maybe some snow-plowing (Chicago did not plow side streets), finding an attorney, or securing a job or city contract. Remember the old phrase, "one hand washes the other?" That's kind of how it worked. Everyone voted Democrat, placed their choice of one candidate in a sign in front of their house, talked up the good deed with the neighbors, walked neighbors over to the precinct on election days, and voted the "right" way.

Mayor Richard J. Daley, sometimes considered the 'last' of big city bosses, served 21 years, when he died in office. There was a twelve year lapse between Daley's, until 1989 when his son, Richard M. Daley took office. Richard served 22 years.

Politics aside, nevertheless, all of America faced the depression. As businesses began failing, the government created the Smoot-Hawley Tariff in 1930 to help protect American companies. This charged a high tax for imports, thereby leading to less trade between America and foreign countries along with some economic retaliation. Does this sound familiar? In addition, the sales tax was slowly implemented by various states. Back in the 1920s, West Virginia was the first state to enact such a tax, and by the end of the 30s, a little over 20 states had grasped the idea and implemented this tax.

Sandi Ludwa

The Dust Bowl

Then there was agriculture and the severe drought conditions. Severe is not strong enough to describe the hardships Americans faced if you lived in parts of Oklahoma, Kansas, Colorado, or Texas in the Great Plain states. Have you ever seen pictures of the Dust Bowl? It was pretty bad. While not a direct cause of the Great Depression, the drought that occurred in the Great Plains in 1930 was so huge that people could not even pay their taxes or other debts and had to sell their farms for pennies, going bankrupt in the process. The Great Plains encompass parts of ten states. The area, aptly nicknamed The Dust Bowl, was the theme of John Steinbeck's *The Grapes of Wrath* and brought it into perspective.

Bugs were relentless, heat was scorching and over 100° on most summer days, and no water or grass for cattle could be found. Cattle were slaughtered rather than having them suffer and starve, and people moved into their storm cellars in an attempt to breathe. Visibility, was zero. If caught out on the plains, it was hopeless. All anyone could do was pray to the good Lord for rain, while in other Mississippi Valley areas, there was flooding.

Neighbors tried to help neighbors and would pool their small change when a foreclosure auction was pending. They would go to these Penny Auctions, keep the bidding low, purchase the property, and return it to the owner.

You must be dreaming...a College Degree?

Schools had severe cutbacks and the school day shortened. There were fewer teachers, larger classes, layoffs, reduced pay, and some schools closed altogether. Some older students preferred staying in school and hanging around, if education was available. There were no jobs, so what else could they do?

In rural areas, there was still the one room schoolhouse and the teachers were not much older than the students. Still, some left school in the eighth grade to help their families. There were no laws forcing school enrollment. College educations were beyond the means and aspirations of most families.

36

Did the Twenties Roar?

We're a bit complacent today when we think about college. There are public community colleges, advance placement, college loans, work-study, scholarships, fellowships, veteran benefits, trade schools and universities, and apprenticeships.

In the 1920s and 1930s, certainly there were colleges. A college education was viewed as making the grade and something to be proud of as so few attained this remarkable achievement. If you were not of the white race, however, prospects to achieving a college education in a public school were poor.

If you were of the right color, admission was not easy. There were tuition fees. Did you learn your Latin or Greek in high school? How about algebra? Did your high school even offer these advanced courses? How about the dreaded entrance testing? There were College Board Tests and the SAT began testing in 1926. Rules, rules, and more rules, as well as fees came forth. Some state schools were technically free but there were often additional health fees, student activity fees, plus room and board, and textbooks. College was not for everyone.

Nevertheless, women became emancipated and in the early 20s many went to college. Freedom from parents, all female dorms, smoking, and parties. Ooh la la! The trend continued throughout the 20s.

There were a little over 122,000 bachelor's degrees awarded in 1930 and approximately 15,000 master's degrees. Schools were still segregated by gender. This continued at many schools until the 60s or so, as well as the language, transfer, and continuing education requirements.

Once the 30s hit, even the large well-endowed private schools couldn't meet financial needs and there were budget cuts which affected salaries and hiring. The New Deal couldn't adapt this area into their plans and public institutions suffered greatly. However, there were work-study programs and numerous buildings erected by the WPA and PWA. There was a drop in enrollment and high drop-out rate. The middle class could no longer afford college.

Sandi Ludwa

We're all in this together

Americans have felt from day one that they were special, entitled, and manifest destiny ruled. American spirit came to its zenith as it was tested in the 30s. People still had their pride and tried to look the best that they could. Although some begged, people got-together and helped one-another. Potlucks and bring a dish to pass were popular and remain so in our present day and age.

Remember when we were back in the eras before Columbus and we viewed the Natives forming tribes? It was for survival, and nothing changed through the centuries. Neighbors helped neighbors, some landlords were lenient, children worked at whatever jobs they could get to help their families, and women took any low-paying job available.

We ate bean sandwiches, make-shift casseroles, chipped beef on toast, mac and cheese, and innovative soups. People ate at home and everyone sat at the dinner table, together. People talked and didn't stare at nonexistent cell phones. It was impolite to read a newspaper at the table, and some families held hands and said grace.

Many of the dishes from hard times spilled into later years and are still popular today. In this century, however, they've been reclassified to a gourmet group. For example, when I was growing up, rice with warm milk was a staple. Now it's a 'a la' recipe with spices, dried fruit, and nuts.

My grandma used to serve wild mushrooms and asparagus that she picked from the county forest preserve. As a kid, I was forced to eat a few bites. She stated that ever since the Depression she foraged. When I think back, it's amazing that people knew what to pick and what to leave alone. I'm awed that none of us perished from a misplaced mushroom or two.

The church pot-luck dinners were a God-send. Men hunted rabbits, fished, and once again many Americans lived closer to the land. There was not an overpopulation of deer or wild turkeys for that matter, but almost everyone hunted. Alligator, anyone? If you've ever had the opportunity to talk to someone who lived through it or heard an account from a friend or relative, you'll realize that the experience lived on forever. Frugality became a way of life, even in good times. The gap between the have and have-nots widened.

"Don't Nickle and Dime Me"

Funny how phrases catch on, this one goes back long before the Great Depression but could be applied to life at this time. Demand for coins dropped and affected the U.S. Mints. (2008 was the second Great Depression and there was a repeat of less demand). Nevertheless, production of various coins was dramatically reduced.

From 1931-33, pennies, nickels, dimes, and quarters were still in demand but coinage was limited as demand dropped. Half dollar coinage was limited and there were no silver dollars put into circulation. Gold coins were not minted. It all seemed to come back to nickels and dimes. For a nickel you could buy an apple and help the guy standing on the street corner, or buy a loaf of bread. For a dime, the prospects were endless, from produce to clothing. How about penny candy? It's always been around.

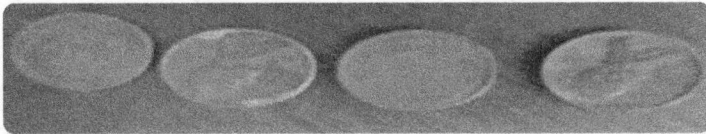

Stretching Pennies

Sandi Ludwa

"Hope springs eternal"....Alexander Pope

Bonus March

We are now living in Hooverville's. Bing Crosby is singing, "Brother Can You Spare a Dime?" We have no money, it's 1932, and the veterans are staging the Bonus March. Unemployed World War II vets are fed-up and marching on Washington for the promised bonuses which were to be paid in 1945. The problem is, they need their bonuses now. Let's put ourselves in their shoes and look back at the situation.

Congress said the pension or bonus, also known as the Tombstone Bonus, would be $1.00 for each day served in the United States or $1.25 if you were in direct combat. The catch was, if you were entitled to more than $50, you had to wait twenty years. The idea of a march on Washington started with a group of vets in Portland, Oregon. It caught momentum and veterans came from everywhere, all across the United States.

The train companies allowed the vets to come from across the nation, without tickets. Once the thousands arrived, they camped out and attempted to meet with the president. Hoover refused to meet with them.

Estimates range that there were anywhere from 12,000 to over 25,000 who came along with wives and children, over a period of two months. Most came dressed in threadbare clothing or in tattered World War I uniforms. Some carried and proudly waved American flags.

The Washington Chief of Police, Pelham D. Glassford, who had been the youngest brigadier general in World War I, sympathized and was able to solicit funds for building materials, food, general supplies, and provide some support for the marchers. He believed in their cause so much that he contributed a significant amount of his own money and found a large number of good people who supported the cause.

Congressional members were still getting paid somewhere around $10,000 a year, and yet they did nothing. There was a vote passed in the House to allow some early settlement but the Patman Bonus Bill didn't pass the Senate. The Democrat Representative from Tennessee, Edward Eslick, died on the House floor while delivering a very passionate speech for the passing of the bill. Congress adjourned, out of respect, and then the House passed the bill. However, the Senate was somewhat unaffected and defeated it.

The vets wanted their money, which would have been approximately $1,000 per veteran. When the bill stalled, the marchers stayed in Washington. Picture the frustration. Nationwide, the newspapers and radio stations brought the plight of the vets to national attention and vets came from all 48 states. Americans, not directly involved in the march, understood the veterans' plight and brought food and provisions to help feed the marchers and their families.

The government did offer to pay transportation to leave and go back home, plus a small daily subsistence allowance. Over 5,000 took advantage of the offer. The others camped and remained in D.C.

Some said the newspapers missed the big issue. Both black and white came together for one common cause...the march. There was no segregation amongst the marchers. Let's meet some of main characters.

General Douglas MacArthur said, "MacArthur smells revolution in the air." MacArthur may have been a great general, but he possessed a trait that many considered strange. He always spoke of himself in the third person. MacArthur was egotistical and opinionated and it came to light when he served until President Truman removed him for insubordination. MacArthur was the Army Chief of Staff.

General Dwight D. Eisenhower, a future president, in 1932 was MacArthur's chief aide and ordered to attend the march and represent the government. Ike had warned MacArthur and advised him to delegate lower ranking troops to handle the situation. He also affirmed there was no authority to follow the marchers across the river if they fled to the huge tent-city that was set up.

Major George S. Patton arrived early and ordered the cavalry troops to mount and follow. They were equipped with gas masks, bayonets, and sabers.

July 5, 1932 arrived. To put an end to the march, the vets were removed by the military under all three of the aforementioned men, Douglas MacArthur, George Patton, and Dwight D. Eisenhower.

This was done brutally and with heavy equipment. Old Tanks which were relics from World War I, infantry, and even a machine gun detachment came thundering down Pennsylvania Avenue as the bonus army fled in terror. MacArthur went beyond presidential orders and followed the men over the Anacostia River, forcing the tent city to be burned.

Meanwhile, the police ensured that all who had been seeking refuge in public buildings were evicted. News broadcasts reported the events to the general public and documentaries went viral. Hoover later stated that many of the marchers were not veterans but communists and criminals. MacArthur added that only around ten percent of the marchers were, in fact, veterans. Several newspapers, however, spoke out against the president. It was the final straw. In 1936, the marchers did receive their pensions.

***

Help was desperately needed and it came from Democrat Franklin Delano Roosevelt, or FDR. The Republicans were reluctant to replace Hoover, but searched for an option. Nevertheless, they could not agree on a strong candidate. Hoover ran again and millions voted for him, although in 1932, FDR, a Democrat, won the election over Hoover by a landslide. This was the greatest political landslide in United States history. FDR obtained 472 electoral votes, and Hoover won 59. There were also candidates running under the Socialist, Communist, Prohibition, Liberty, and Socialist Labor Parties. There are various opinions on why people voted Republication for Hoover after all the country was going through. Would you have voted for Hoover?

Various opinions emerged. One was black voters knew the Democrat Party was one of racism and FDR said little on the issue despite his active campaigning throughout the country. The party's history showed it did little for all Americans in the South.

Another was the fact that patronage jobs were widely distributed in major cities with huge black and immigrant populations. Many of the free giveaways were also sponsored by both parties in the large cities.

There were those who felt abandoned by the Democrats for much too long and retained their early Republican roots. Others, favored extending temperance, which Hoover supported. Yet, there were other loyal party members who believed Hoover would implement a "New Deal" and they continued to be creatures of habit and voted as they had for decades.

Hoover became a strong critic of FDR and the depression continued for another eight years. He returned to politics in the 1950s and served on commissions under both President Truman and Eisenhower. He passed away in 1964 at age 90.

You be the judge. Was Hoover unfortunate enough to be president at the wrong time? Could another more powerful person have turned the tide? Were his policies poor or not strong enough to lead Americans out of this hole? Once again, I believe we need to know all of the facts and judge by past standards and not those of today.

Even though FDR claimed a sensational victory, all was not well. Teddy Roosevelt's Oyster Bay relatives despised FDR because he was a Democrat. Today's politics are nothing new and families still fight about political parties. His two most spiteful opponents were Teddy's daughter, Alice Longworth and Teddy's son, Theodore Roosevelt, Jr. who had his own political ambitions. Nevertheless, FDR won the election.

Chapter 4

"Happy Days Are Here Again"

Hoover continually pestered Roosevelt to come into office during the "interregnum" or transition period (in Latin, it was the "time between the kings). He sought Roosevelt's involvement in many of the issues which were becoming more and more challenging day by day.

Hoover did try a last-ditch effort to revive the economy in 1932 with the Reconstruction Finance Corporation (RFC) which gave federal loans to banks, railroads, and businesses. It didn't help because the money went to large banks and corporations with collateral, not the common man. All of the allocated money was never spent.

In the meantime, Roosevelt declined to take part in any decisions during the interregnum period and used these months to work on his "New Deal" and assemble the strongest cabinet he could. These were knowledgeable people from diverse backgrounds. The members of his Cabinet are listed with a few of their distinctions and accomplishments:

• Senator Cordell Hull of Tennessee, Secretary of State – born in a log cabin, recipient of the Nobel Peace Prize, and longest in office Secretary of State ever – 11 years.

• William H. Woodin of New York, Secretary of the Treasury was a Republican. He resigned within a year because of poor health.

• Former Governor George H. Dern of Utah as Secretary of War fought for social welfare, public education, and tax reform. He was a former Utah Governor and in office with FDR for close to three years until his death.

- Senator Claude A. Swanson of Virginia, Secretary of the Navy was an attorney and senator, and FDR's leading critic of the New Deal.

- Homer S. Cummings, Attorney General (replacing Thomas J. Walsh who died two days before the inauguration. He was a Progressive, an attorney, and peacemaker. He tried to reunite the Democrats in 1924, when the KKK was an issue within the party.

- Postmaster General James A. Farley of New York was one of the first Irish Catholics to enter politics on a national level. He also strove for closer diplomatic relationships with the Pope during FDR's administration. He had a falling out with FDR as he opposed the breaking of the two-term presidency rule. He later became a power in New York as a Democrat Boss.

- Henry A. Wallace, a farmer from Iowa, Secretary of Agriculture was an agricultural expert and later became a one-term vice president under FDR but was opposed by southerners.

- Harold L. Ickes of Chicago, Secretary of the Interior for thirteen years and implemented much of the New Deal.

- Secretary of Commerce, Daniel C. Roper was a teacher and politician and major New Deal player.

- One woman, Frances Perkins, Secretary of Labor was a sociologist and worked for workers' rights. She served twelve years as Secretary of Labor, and has the record for it.

There they are, The Brain Trust. They were respected because they were extremely knowledgeable, educated, and well-informed people from every field, and represented a cross-section of Americana. We live in an age where few dare to cross party lines. Those that take a view from the other side of the fence, often sacrifice their careers when their own party shuns them.

FDR, however, crossed party-lines and placed those whom he believed to be the best for the country, regardless of the criticisms and bad press he received. The press voiced its opinions and didn't state the facts and allow the public to decide right or wrong. They made the decision for the people. Keep in mind, in the 30s, it was extremely rare for a president to take such bold steps.

Three members of the incoming Cabinet, Secretaries Woodin, Wallace, and Ickes, were Republicans while the other six advisors were Democrats. Frances Perkins became the first female in history to serve on a Cabinet.

Roosevelt was in a difficult situation for a new president and could be compared to Abe Lincoln's arrival in the midst of a catastrophic situation. Of FDR's selections, the appointments of Dern and Farley, like that of Woodin and Perkins, were regarded as very personal. When Roosevelt went fishing, he truly went fishing. He turned the government over to them completely, and trusted their decisions. There were assassination attempts and sometimes fate played a hand.

In 1933, two weeks before the official inauguration, FDR went to Miami. He had just completed his speech from the back seat of his Buick, when numerous shots were heard. FDR was not struck. Instead Chicago Mayor Anton Cermak was shot six times and died. There was speculation.

The murderer was Giuseppe Zangara, an unemployed bricklayer. Since Zangara was short, he stood on a stool in order to view FDR. One bystander stated she had jerked his hand and that was the reason FDR was spared. Yet others state it was because Roosevelt couldn't stand up. The public still didn't realize that fact.

Nevertheless, Cermak was killed and four others injured. FDR remained calm, ordered the driver to pick up the wounded, and held Cermak until they arrived at the hospital. FDR refused all attempts to be taken from the scene and removed to safety. The public was elated and many agreed they had voted correctly, by placing FDR into office.

Five days after his inauguration, FDR called a special meeting of Congress to get the ball rolling and start a New Deal. His programs amounted to what some called, 'a welfare state, welfare capitalism, or fascism.' The administration was forced to work within many constraints and found if something couldn't be done they would work around it or figure out a better sales pitch to get the job completed.

And the Bonus Marchers? When FDR took office, approximately 3,000 of the marchers came back to Washington and lived in a tent city. Eleanor Roosevelt visited with them and there was a saying that Hoover sent our Army while Roosevelt sent his wife. Nevertheless, FDR offered jobs through his New Deal programs and the majority took them. Yes, there were still those who considered the wages inadequate and refused the work.

FDR viewed payment to veterans differently than his usual helping-hand behavior. In 1935, the Bonus Bill was reintroduced under the Patman Greenback Bonus Bill and vetoed by FDR who believed it wasn't a relief bill and by passing it, would be showing favoritism to one group. He strongly believed other groups would demand the same, if the bill passed and said the vets shouldn't be granted any more privileges and treated any differently than any other American citizens.

In 1935, the Second New Deal began. It was more liberal and more controversial. In June 1936, the Wright Patman Bill was reintroduced once again and vets started receiving early payment when redeeming their certificates. More than 80% were immediately redeemed while those who waited kept accumulating interest. FDR, however, vetoed the bill but it passed with the support of veterans, one was Senator Harry S. Truman and a more liberal Congress.

The Hoover Dam & That 'Damn Dog'

Six construction companies secured rigid contracts; together they pooled their resources to meet the high dollar performance bond. First, they blasted the canyon walls and formed tunnels. Men worked in 100 plus degree temperatures, faced carbon monoxide, dust, and the desert. Then the walls had to be cleared. Men worked at heights over 800 feet from the floor of the structure. Then, they built a powerplant.

During the depression, workers along with their families, came to the area hoping to become employed. Many lived in Ragtown or Las Vegas. Conditions were poor, and they faced the scorching heat averaging 120°, contrasted by cold and frigid nights. The land was desert, and many died.

Boulder City became a Godsend for many. Built by the six construction companies and the Bureau of Reclamation, Boulder City emerged as a model city.

Men had to conform to the demands. Boulder City was dry (no alcohol) and there would be no gambling. I know what you're thinking. America was under Prohibition, so what's the big deal?

Well, Las Vegas, being Las Vegas, simply ignored the whole prohibition thing. Gambling, prostitution, and anything illegal still existed. Most people even supported a petition to legally allow alcohol. But, it was of no matter, because Vegas did whatever Vegas wanted to do, legal or not. It was still Sin City.

At any rate, the dam was completed twenty-two months ahead of schedule, dedicated by Franklin D. Roosevelt in 1936, and it was a masterpiece. Hoover wasn't invited to the ceremony as the Roosevelt administration believed Hoover had contributed little to its completion. FDR's Secretary of the Interior disliked Hoover and renamed the dam back to its original designation, the Boulder Dam. In 1947, however, under the Truman Administration, once again its name was changed to the Hoover Dam.

Initially, the city offered no school buildings, hospital, and few businesses. Designated housing was granted by workers' status of importance. Business owners hoping to locate in the city, had to undergo strict character checks and balances. Eventually, a hospital was erected and there was no longer a 33 mile transport for urgent medical attention, however, women were not admitted until years later.

The story of the Boulder or Hoover Dam, whichever you want to call it, is not complete without a story about the Damn Dog or Dog of the Dam, "Nig," whose name is never spoken as it is considered offensive in today's society. The part-lab animal was born in 1932 and soon became a trusted and welcome member of the crew.

Nig was no ordinary dog! He could climb ladders, and often followed the men into the tunnels. The much loved and treasured dog was spoiled by all and overfed to the point the town doctor issued a news article telling people to stop feeding him a bad diet.

Soon, our Damn Dog was getting meals from the commissary, paid for by the men. He would stand in line with the men, who would unwrap his food, and then all would go back to work together, including our dog. As society goes, a plaque was erected but taken down because it was considered controversial. Another remembrance was finally placed in 1979, without the cherished dog's name.

On a recent trip, I asked about our Damn Dog. The ranger pointed out the general location but gave little information on the amazing animal, nor would mention his name. The High Scaler Restaurant at Hoover Dam, sells half-pound hot dogs which they refer to as "Damn Dogs."

On my recent trip to Hoover Dam, I found the plaque:

The Hoover Dam construction crew's mascot was found as a puppy by workers at the construction camp. This dog traveled to and from the damsite with them and spent his days visiting the many work areas. On February 21, 1941, the life of this devoted animal came to an end when a truck under which he was sleeping rolled over him. The grave below was completed by workers later that same day.

Sandi Ludwa

More Programs Emerge

The Emergency Banking Act in March 1933, took effect almost immediately after FDR was inaugurated was perhaps one of the most-bold. All banks in our country closed for a week and reopened with funds protected by the Federal Deposit Insurance Corp.

Banks returned all of their gold to the Federal Reserve. You couldn't redeem your dollars for gold, export it, or hoard it. The following year, the Gold Reserve Act prohibited private ownership of gold, except if you had a federal license. The United States held the majority of the world's gold. It wasn't until 1971, however, under the Nixon Administration, that we completely abandoned our gold standard. At any rate, when the banks closed, it was still the Depression and it was a day that money stopped.

Could you still run a 'tab' at your local store? Could you even afford a shoeshine or taxicab ride?

Since the beginnings of our great nation, there was never a guarantee of return once you deposited your funds. Remember the old ? When the bandits took the money, it was gone. Roosevelt reassured the nation in a fireside chat that it was safer to deposit money in a bank rather than placing it under a mattress.

Then there was the Securities Exchange Commission that oversaw the stock market. It took a while to accomplish its purpose to restore confidence, trust, and honesty after a long period of corruption.

The Federal Emergency Relief Administration was another dramatic undertaking. Henry Hopkins ran it with billions of dollars that created jobs through the Civil Works Administration (CWA) and the Public Works Administration (PWA). The PWA built the Lincoln Tunnel, and FERA completed the Overseas Highway which ran the length of the Florida Keys. People built schools, hospitals, courthouses, and bridges.

There was the CCC (Civil Conservation Corp) for unemployed youth which gave us parks, planted trees, and fought forest fires. Initially, men had to be between 18 and 26 years of age and single, but rules changed to include war vets. These men reforested by planting billions of trees, especially in vast areas of the Dust Bowl. They built fire roads, worked to control insects, developed campgrounds, and controlled flooding, to name a few.

Workers earned $30 a month and had to send money home to their families. Thirty dollars would be equivalent to approximately $585 in today's dollars. Take into account the cost of living in 1933.

The WPA and CCC established the Smoky Mountain National Park. Land acquisition and construction of the Blue Ridge Parkway began, was halted by the war, and finally completed (1987). Most sections were open for decades.

When I venture out into this country, it seems there is never an occasion when there is not something that still exists that was erected or sown by one of these agencies. Examples are structures in our state and national parks. We can be thankful for the trails, over 3 billion trees that were planted, re-seeded land, and the government's prevention of soil erosion.

Our First Minimum Wage Laws

Americans complain about minimum wage laws, but before 1933, there was none. The National Recovery Act (NRA) regulated prices, working conditions, and the right to bargain. No folks, it does not refer to the National Rifle Association. It set prices in 41 industries with minimum wages from .25 to .45 an hour and maximum work hours weekly of 45 hours. Two million employers signed up. People endorsed it which included garment workers, women, and the country. Nevertheless, it was a failure and in 1935 the Supreme Court ruled it unconstitutional. It contained no enforcement and labor problems continued

There were labor unions in existence and the A.F. of L. and C.I.O. were powerful. While some struck, others staged sit-ins and 1937 was a record year. Workers at the major auto producers, e.g., Chrysler, Ford, General Motors, sat in when the companies refused to sign contracts. The sit-ins were popular because companies found it difficult to remove workers who were on the job, sitting.

Why did they rebel? There was still animosity about the right to organize and the issues of wages and hours. Many workers, however, did not have the large umbrella of an A.F. of L. or C.I.O. and belonged to much smaller unions. During these troubled times, it always meant taking a chance on your future livelihood.

When did we start helping farmers?

The AAA aka, the Agricultural Adjustment Act, enacted in 1933, paid farmers subsidies not to produce. It was supply, demand, and waste. As pigs were butchered, milk poured on the ground, and oranges and apples placed in kerosene, the public looked on in disbelief. In theory, this would benefit the farmers and not the consumers who would pay higher prices since less existed.

People were still starving and tenant farmers, sharecroppers, and small farms were pushed to the point of starvation while the owners pocketed the profits. At first, the owners were to pay a portion of their earnings which they obtained for not producing to tenants and sharecroppers, but this soon stopped.

This turned into a disaster. America was soon importing. The Act continued as farmers lobbied to keep it, but in 1938 the Supreme Court declared it was unconstitutional. Portions of it were re-enacted and still exist today. We are now in the twenty-first century and farm subsidies still exist. However, the Trump Administration has proposed drastic cuts in the program and a Democrat contender stated anyone can be a farmer.

Perhaps, John Steinbeck gave one of the insights into agrarian culture and the Great Depression, in his novel, *The Grapes of Wrath,* which was published in 1939. The book is always recommended when someone asks about the era. It depicts the Dust Bowl and Great Depression, bringing this generation into an understanding of what conditions really existed.

NIRA and TVA and Government pay cuts?

The NIRA, National Industrial Reconstruction Administration, involved wage controls. More money was given for working less and the object was to hire more people. A form of this policy exists today in France. Nevertheless, the NIRA is viewed as a disaster in the United States in the 1930s.

The (TVA), Tennessee Valley Authority provided electricity and jobs and was a huge success, and it still exists today. Travel through the Smokies to its headquarters in Knoxville. During your journey, note the great dams, realize there is flood control, and that the TVA is an economic boom to a large area.

When was the last time we heard about pay cuts in government? FDR ensured that there was a Congressional pay cut to $8500 from $10,000.

There were those conservatives who said the New Deal went too far. Then, there were the liberals who said it didn't go far enough. Any opinions?

Golden Gate Bridge Completed 1937

A Government-owned Utopian Society?

Another development from this administration was the building of government cities. This Utopian idea would display a variety of housing from duplexes, townhomes, apartment complexes, and single-family dwellings. There were three cities to be built and they were called the "greenbelt cities." Putting up three communities from scratch took from 1936 until 1938.

The plan, under the New Deal's Resettlement Administration, was devised as yet another means to provide work for Americans, resettle displaced Americans, and establish preplanned exemplary communities. In these ideal environments, the government hoped to bring together people of various faiths, occupations, and those who could contribute positively to the communities. These communities would be self-sufficient and create much needed jobs. As the Dust Bowl continued with no end in sight, people left California and the Great Plains by the millions. This massive program was another attempt to end this Great Depression.

If we look to the present, during the last two decades, hundreds of thousands have also left California. These are usually middle and lower class while those moving into the state usually have higher incomes. Nevertheless, more are leaving that immigrating. The reasons cited now-a-days for exiting the state have nothing to do with agriculture. They are a high cost of living, political climate, and taxes. So much for "California Here I Come." (1925 song written by Buddy DeSylva and Joseph Meyer).

Back in 1936, however, the plan was to create three communities. Two were suburbs and one rural. They were to be walkable, offer ample public facilities, and become safe and secure environments. While providing plenty of green space, these communities would stand as models for America and typify the American Dream.

Residents were closely-screened. The plans were pre-runners to our housing projects of today with guidelines on who could participate. There were income minimums and maximums and residences were to be considered affordable for all who resided in them. Community buildings, stores, and facilities were cooperatively run.

The three cities were Greenhills, Ohio (rural), Greenbelt, Maryland (near D.C), and Greendale, Wisconsin (near Milwaukee). They were built on undeveloped land. The vision was for hundreds of communities to be built. It never happened.

In the late 1940s and early 1950s, the government finally divested itself from owning property and homes were put up for sale to the public. Many were destroyed because they had been neglected over the years and were beyond saving. Our government simply couldn't afford to maintain them.

Were these government cooperative communities successful? It depends upon your point of view. Were they inclusive to consider all Americans in an initial screening? No, they didn't allow blacks. Building had cost overages because heavy machinery was off-limits in order to make work for the unemployed. Locations were too far from the major cities and transportation was nil. Conservatives believed they were too socialistic with the many cooperative ventures.

Others view them as successful because the communities exist today. Homes have been updated and modernized and considered historic. Current residents enjoy their homes. During the Depression they were affordable and comfortable residences for many Americas and provided the green space in a safe and unpolluted environment. It was another attempt to alleviate the struggles during our Great Depression.

Escape for a Few Hours?

Despite changes to reconstruct and save the nation from this ongoing depression, there was another side. In 1933, the Century of Progress Exhibition opened in Chicago. Promoters were worried that their years of planning, preparation, and building, would go bust since this was the height of the depression. However, by the end of its run, over 22 million people had visited the fair. It was located on what is called Northerly Island which later was home to Meigs Field (closed in 2003) and the present McCormick Place.

Promoters knew that they needed exhibits going above and beyond. They treated fairgoers with glitz. It featured the latest in auto, rail, invention, and manufacturing. It brought a sort of Utopia to fair-goers who could look beyond their present dismal lives and into the promised future. Future celebrities such as Judy Garland presented acts on the evening midway while Sally Rand displayed it all in her striptease. Free publicity is good and was welcomed back in the 30s as much as it is in the 2020s. Sally was arrested several times for indecency but soon released and the public was drawn in and curious to see the show because of this helping hand to boost sales.

The fair displayed exhibits which would be frowned upon in this twenty-first century. There were dwarfs, blacks, incubator babies, and untold curiosities. Animals, architecture, foods, crafts, and temptations which awed the public continued through November when there was a dysentery outbreak. However, the fair reopened in the following year to run another five months. When it closed, it was deemed a financial success for its backers, despite the Great Depression which consumed America. For those who could scrape-up enough for the admission, it was a temporary escape and brought some hope for the future.

Movies were popular. In 1928 Walt Disney produced the first Mickey Mouse cartoon and cheap movies were an escape for everyone. Millions of Americans scraped together their coins and went every week. The price was usually around .25 to .35 and there were a lot of choices. Should we see James Cagney in a gangster movie? How about Clark Gable, Bette Davis, or the dancing duo of Fred Astaire and Ginger Rogers?

In 1937, Disney gave us *Snow White* and in 1939 it was the debut of *Gone With the Wind.* Some towns even offered free outdoor movies. America loved Shirley Temple and Clark Gable's wife Carol Lombard.

As with anything fun and popular, there were strict rules in filming movies. Twin beds for couples, short kisses only, no racial mixing, and how about the Catholic Legion of Decency, which rated movies? Ratings went from X and Indecent to Family Recommended. However, if the Catholic recommendations were too strict for you, and you wanted the 'inside info' you would read *Photoplay* Magazine.

If you couldn't afford a film, listening to the radio was also a pastime. Tune into the *Green Hornet* or the *Lone Ranger.* We would be 'hooked' and eager to hear the next episode. Would the villain throw the heroine over the cliff? Would the train run over the beautiful lady before she was saved? How did we survive? What if you missed an episode?

Participation in sports, family board games, reading aloud, and jigsaw puzzles were popular. Younger kids played hide-and-seek and drop the handkerchief while the elders played pinochle, bridge, or whist. Monopoly and Scrabble were always hits.

Who could forget H.G. Well's *War of the Worlds?* It sent America into panic. Were there really aliens invading planet Earth? Heaven forbid! H. G. Wells did run the ire of many, including William Randolph Hearst, especially when he wrote, directed, and produced *Citizen Kane.* He took information that was said to incriminate both Hearst and Pulitzer, the two newspaper tycoons. The power of the press retaliated and Hearst outlawed any mention of the movie in his syndicate of papers.

Did the Twenties Roar?

Do you like to dance? Marathon dancing had been going on since the twenties and continued its popularity. If you didn't dance, you could go and observe for free! If you paired up with your favorite date and tested how long you could remain on the dancefloor dancing, you might win some money or some fantastic prizes.

Some of these events went on for weeks and there were strict rules for remaining in the contest. If your knees even touched the floor, you were disqualified. Sleep deprivation was the number one enemy and hallucinations were not uncommon. Professional dancers pretending to be amateurs abounded. Then there were the hired actors and actresses who started commotions to gain the limelight and continue public interest.

The unscrupulous promoters were not uncommon. They would often enlist the support of some not for profit organization, promising a share of the profits, and then skip town before bills were paid and prizes passed out. Nonetheless, this was inexpensive fun. There were raffles, free food, and side entertainment such as fake weddings.

Many cities began outlawing these dance events, calling these contests "immoral, physically dangerous, and breeding sin." As humiliating, shameful, and dangerous as they were, the public flocked to the dance halls. It was rumored that people actually collapsed and died while trying to win the big prize! Marathon dancing did help the economy and large cities drew them. Money flowed for advertising, vendors, licensing fees, nurses, judges, and the hired contestants that usually claimed the 'rigged' prize.

****

For the younger set, however, dates were usually double dates. There was always a curfew in order to curtail any hanky-panky such as 'necking' outside of the ice cream shop. Playing cards, dominoes, or hanging out at someone's home with mom and dad present was always suggested. As the younger set got a bit older, mom would give some tips to both sons and daughters.

For the ladies, remember to never reapply makeup in his rearview mirror, and don't chew gum. For the gentlemen, be on time for your date and do go overboard and be super-polite to her parents. The most important rule of all was 'no kissing on the first date.'

People followed fads. There were the "flagpole sitters." All you had to do was climb up a pole and sit on it...maybe for a month or two! How about swallowing goldfish? For boys it was the soap box derby, a great spectator and participant pastime.

Americans looked forward to hearing and seeing the filming of the 1936 Summer Olympics in Germany. This turned out to be a low point in history and a premonition of what was to come. The Olympics were Hitler's chance to promote his goals of racial supremacy. Although many boycotted, American Jesse Owens still won four gold medals in competition, showing color doesn't matter in athletic competitions.

There is a famous quote, which no one can prove who first said it. It could have been Abraham Lincoln or P.T. Barnum, or dozens of others. I will attribute it to "someone once said" the following which goes like this:

"You can please some of the people all of the time, you can please all of the people some of the time, but you can't please all of the people all of the time."

Even though the majority loved FDR, his style and demeanor, and his attempts to hoist Americans out of the depression, many said he was a dictator. His adversaries and the disillusioned protested against him, but he kept trying. FDR said, "If I fail, I will become the last president." He looked to give future generations a great land and country to be proud of, which is our America. Some of the administration's attempts helped substantially or little, while some were defeated before they were even announced. If something entirely failed when implemented, FDR persisted with more of his New Deals.

Among FDR's critics were some that were very powerful and caused him many problems. One was Louisiana Senator, Huey Long. Long was corrupt, took bribes, and was assassinated in 1935. He kept a box on his desk which was simply labeled, 'donations.'

Another friend turned foe was a Catholic Priest. In 1926, Father Charles Edward Coughlin broadcasted the first of his weekly sermons on public radio. In 1928, Catholic Al Smith lost the presidential election and many

Catholics and Irish Catholics were disenchanted and looked for a new voice. They found a hero in Coughlin.

By 1930, his powerful sermons went off religion and onto the economy and politics. People were obsessed with the oncoming Depression and Coughlin offered his prospective on the world. He was a huge success, received over 80,000 letters a week, and formed the National Union for Social Justice.

Coughlin thought FDR was like him and would "drive the money changers from the temple." He said "Roosevelt or Ruin" but when FDR didn't fund radical reforms that Coughlin believed in, he turned against FDR in the 1936 election. When Coughlin started expounding anti-Semitism remarks and praised Hitler and Mussolini, FDR abruptly ended his ties with the priest. Coughlin was a very powerful force, but eventually, was forced off the radio and lost a majority of his following.

Despite failures, criticisms, and foes, FDR continued with his plan, if something doesn't work, try something else. He gave a speech in May 1932 at Oglethorpe University in Atlanta, which summed up this philosophy in one single paragraph:

"The country needs and, unless I mistake its temper, the country demands bold persistent experimentation. It is common sense to take a method and trip it. If it fails, admit it frankly and try another. But above all, try something."

Franklin Delano Roosevelt

Capitalism was saved. FDR continued to be charming and charismatic, and the public overall loved him. He listened to people's ideas. In the 1930s there was no internet, Google, or Twitter. On Sunday evenings everyone gathered around the radio for his broadcast or Fireside Chats which won over many American's hearts and souls. His dog Falla (Fa La), a Scottish terrier, was adored and newspapers reported on the canine's daily activities.

FDR gave a speech to the Teamsters Union in 1944, stating it was alright to insult him, his wife or son, but now they criticized Falla. FDR continued that he nor his family resented attacks, but Falla did resent attacks, took them personally, and hoped they would stop. The dog was given to him by Daisy Suckley (Sook-lee) a distant cousin. There have been many stories about Daisy and FDR but I'll leave any investigation to you.

FDR did have a mistress, Lucy Mercer, Eleanor's secretary. In 1916, Eleanor had found love letters. Nevertheless, Eleanor remained FDR's closest confidante and his eyes, ears, and legs. He listened to her suggestions. She knew the American people and FDR understood the situations. Eleanor believed that in order to understand a state of affairs from someone else's point of view, you had to place yourself in their shoes. She knew Franklin was no different and had his whole-hearted attention.

Eleanor threatened to leave FDR at one time but since Sara Delano held the purse-strings, the idea disappeared. Eleanor stayed married on two conditions: he break off the affair with Lucy Mercer and she and FDR would not cohabit in the bedroom. However, he and Lucy never stopped seeing each other. There were also many other important and influential women who shaped his ideas: Missey LeHand, Daisy Suckley, and Eleanor.

It's difficult to gage how many emails, letters, and gifts our presidents receive today. Needless to say, most are deleted, discarded, unread, and go unanswered. Times were different in the 1930s. FDR and Eleanor received up to 8,000 letters per day. Eleanor read and answered thousands of them individually with the help of her secretaries. She often stayed up until late in the evening, reading.

Throughout the administration, most didn't know about the intense pain FDR experienced daily because of his infantile paralysis (polio). He was stricken in summer 1921. An epidemic raged in New York but FDR was struck at their summer home, Campobello in Maine. This was totally unexpected and FDR was paralyzed from the waist down.

Family and friends expected him to give up politics, retire, and fade into the sunset. Not Roosevelt, whose strong will and determination carried him through. He was a fighter and resented that anyone should think of him as half a man. He resolved that this illness would not change his life plans – to become President of the United States.

FDR had to lock his braces in order to maintain some control, which was extremely painful. It was a major affair just to stand up. His specially built auto with hand controls was a God-send. The American public never knew, or wanted to know, throughout his administrations.

Did the Twenties Roar?

If FDR was in the White House, he was already seated at the table before anyone arrived. How different life is today with media having to know every detail. There were rules for the press on photography and no one complained or filed lawsuits. There were no photographs or images in wheelchairs. If someone dared to capture the moment, the film was confiscated.

So, who was Eleanor? What was the first-lady doing? Slowly she evolved into the respected woman we remember. She became a legend and was never idle. El not only advised FDR as to what was going on in the world, but ventured out on her own, met people, took stock of the situations, and made major changes. She came out of her shell, looked around, and became dominant in women's rights and civil rights. She held women only press conferences since FDR only allowed men.

Eleanor worked with Lorena Hickok, her devoted friend and an innovative journalist. There was a questionable relationship, which raised eyebrows when some of their daily correspondence came to light. She was "Hick, darling." Nevertheless, Lorena inspired Eleanor and helped her develop self-assurance, which El had lacked in her role as first lady. The first lady had grown up in a very dysfunctional household, which is an interesting story in itself.

Lorena and Eleanor did something that would be unheard of in today's world. They took a month-long trip to the Eastern United States without the secret service. Initially, most people didn't recognize Eleanor. It didn't take long, however, that her frequent traveling elevated her one of the best-known and memorable women in the world.

Eleanor also wrote a daily newspaper column, "My Day." Have you ever read a book or article that you couldn't put down and wanted to go on reading? The word was that many women loved the column and couldn't wait to read the next issue.

Eleanor's self-confidence and strength continued to grow throughout her life. She is credited with many quotes that she learned from early childhood. Two of my favorite on empowerment are:

" Nobody can make you feel inferior without your consent."

"In the long run, we shape our lives, and we shape ourselves. The process never ends until we die. And the choices we make are ultimately our own responsibility."

Another thing happened during FDR's first term. The Twenty-first Amendment was enacted. It repealed prohibition. All of a sudden, in the cities there was a great demand for beer licenses, fast and furious!

Chapter 5

Recovery? Or is it?

Summary of the 30s and into the 40s

Americans were at their lowest low, covered with Hoover Blankets, living in Hooverville's, and barely getting enough to eat with Hoover Stew. As our stomachs rumbled, we were unemployed, underemployed, homeless, and experiencing everyday hopelessness. We appreciated the little joys in life. Maybe it was a fancy desert, a piece of penny candy, a thoughtful word from a stranger, a movie, a cup of coffee and a donut, a night with a roof over our heads, or whatever could lessen our constant everyday pain. Along came Franklin D. Roosevelt, from a wealthy family, and a Democrat. He married Anna Eleanor Roosevelt, Teddy Roosevelt's niece and FDR's own fifth cousin who had been once removed.

FDR put together an all-star team and introduced the New Deal. He believed if something didn't work the first time, try and try again. He introduced massive legislation to drag Americans out of depression. Some worked and some didn't. Most Americans never knew that FDR suffered from Polio and could barely stand-up. No reporter dared to confront the president on this issue.

He had lots of enemies and the press and radio were not always kind. In fact, FDR believed the majority were out to get him. There were hundreds of editorials and articles against his policies and he and William Randolph Hearst battled. He fought back with the airwaves through Federal rules and regulations and licensing. Soon, media changed its tune. He fought with the Supreme Court, Western Union, the ACLU, and the list goes on. When things went poorly, he started government investigations of individuals and corporations.

Overall, the public adored him and he retained an abiding faith in the future. If we look back at only pictures, he was always smiling.

The Depression, however, was still with us. 1938 Was another election year and there were still ten million unemployed. The Democrats lost 72 seats in the House of Representatives and 7 in the Senate. In 1940 FDR ran for an unprecedented third term and promised no intervention in the War. He retained support from the Solid South, labor unions, urban political machines, and ethnic voters as he ran against Republican Wendell Willkie. FDR received 449 votes from the Electoral College to Willkie's 82.

FDR and Willkie ran against other parties: Socialist, Communist, Prohibition, and Socialist Labor. Yes folks, the Prohibition Party was still around. Needless to say, the other parties received no electoral votes. Colorado, Indiana, Iowa, Kansas, Maine, Michigan, Nebraska, North Dakota, South Dakota, and Vermont went to Willkie with Michigan right on the line with only 1% of the total votes favoring Willkie.

****

If we looked at magazines in 1939, we wouldn't realize the turmoil going on in America and the rest of the world. I reviewed *Life Magazine*, the January 9, 1939 issue, Vol 6, No. 2. It divided the articles into sections for: Events, Photo Essay, Art, Science, Sports, Movies, and Modern Living.

Some of the articles were: "Winston Churchill: The Peter Pan of British Politics," and "Winter's First Big Blizzard Batters Buffalo." I skipped over the pictures and stories about the $8,000 debutante ball.

After reviewing the ads for: "the Mimeograph Machine, DeSoto, America's Smartest Low-Priced Car, Wake up your Liver Bile, Kreml Removes Dandruff – Checks falling hair, and Bromo-Seltzer," I found: "How Every Woman Can Make Her own Dress Form," something not to be missed!

Such was our lives in the 30s. Turn the page to the 40s…

Wasn't the Great War supposed to be the last?

Recovery is almost certain when there is a war, and here is where we end. December 7, 1941, "a day that will live in infamy" brought reluctance to an end. Franklin Delano Roosevelt went to Congress, stated the phrase that will live forever, and Congress declared war.

We entered the world-wide conflict and the war-time economy flourished. As our men and women went overseas, worked in wartime industries, and supported the cause, once again our great country recovered. We thought World War I, the Great War, would be our last but little did we know...

"America the Beautiful"

Sandi Ludwa

www.ingramcontent.com/pod-product-compliance
Lightning Source LLC
Chambersburg PA
CBHW021218020426
42331CB00003B/367